# THE POWER OF IMPLEMENTATION

**THE MISSING LINK**
BETWEEN
**CORPORATE TRAINING & SALES TARGETS**

ANAND CHHABRA

THE IMPLEMENTATION SPECIALIST SHARES HIS SECRETS

BEEJA HOUSE

**ISBN**: 978-93-95266-12-3 (Paperback)

Published by: Beeja House

First Printing Edition 2023

Author Email: anandchhabra@borntowin.co.in

**www.borntowin.co.in**

# Acknowledgement


*The purpose of writing this book is to help Individuals, Teams and Enterprises succeed in their endeavours – to achieve the explosive growth they dream of and make it into a lifelong practice.*

*The brilliant marketing model developed by Akshar Yadav helped me to become a Marketer! Keep the high energy going!*

*Vinay Agarwal and Pradeep Malhotra helped in implementing the model in my business with their guidance, tips, and critique – I couldn't have finished the book without their valuable input. I don't require support pillars in my life anymore! I do require such lovely friends!*

*Vinod & Bankim Mitra added shine to my effort. Keep your axes sharp!*

# Contents



born towin®

learning services pvt. ltd

*Gudiya brought a lot of love to our lives, making our journey together fun.*
*Keep smiling!!!*

# Chapter 1

## The Issues

*"There is no sarcasm in Born to Win sessions; hence, participants gave 100% to the sessions. Nothing is impossible; every problem has a solution.*
*'I Can' attitude has become the 'We Can' attitude. Major interpersonal issues got settled in the organisation.*
*"Inter and Intra Team bickering has reduced, and Team members recognise the strengths of each other.*
*"Detailing to the last level has improved. Plans include Projections and Action Points. Execution is not being taken as a one-time operation but as a process that is being put in place.*
*"I have now started delegating more.*
*"I start my work on a happy note and share it with everyone.*
*"Activity Management Grid has brought more clarity in my work and reduced my stress."*

***Sanjay Sathu, COO TATA Teleservices (Regional Sales Team)***

- Have you, of late, been worried about stagnating sales figures, falling profit margins and high churn rate of salespersons in your organisation?
- Have the recent events in the economy derailed the journey of your organisation?
- Do you find that:
    - The best strategies designed by you have not been able to help grow your sales figures fast enough.
    - Your people operate from a comfort zone and cannot push your organisation's big goals.

- Your people often work at cross-purpose and are not working towards the organisational goals.
- There is much finger-pointing and blaming each other for non-achievement.
- There is constant firefighting.

And, you have long been searching for that magic solution that delivers the results—that you desire secretly—assured, measurable and sustained?
Is your sales team 25+ and your turnover Rs. 25+ Crore?

***Read on... Continue going through this study... It is meant for you...***

***Bajaj Capital Case Study***

*Bajaj Capital has a unique tradition of supporting the stragglers in their Sales Team – they never ask them to leave. Instead, they provide extra support through training and mentoring.*
*The Vice President, Human Resources, was intrigued by our claim of delivery on assured results.*
*Born To Win was thrown a challenge for their team of 20: "Double their average monthly performance in six months – take their average monthly bonus earnings from 2.36 to 4."*
*At the end of six months, participants' average monthly bonus earnings went up to 4.97. The maximum bonus earned by a Sales Executive, in a single month, during this period was 49.*

# Chapter 2

## *The Analysis*

*"I used to struggle with 'always loaded', no time for family and missed timelines. By 'Aggregating Time to 168 Hours' & using 'Activity Management Grid', I could find time for my Wife & Self. In a week, I allocated 12 hours for taking my Wife out, 5 for Myself, and 42 to Sleep.*

*"Similarly, in my workplace, in a week, I allocated 12 hours for Planning; Review, 12 hours; Market work, 20 hours; Meetings, 14 hours; Travel, 18 hours and Other Routine work, 33 hours.*

*"My team helped by accepting the delegation of routine tasks such as MIS, Project Management, Training and Motivational Talks. For my planning activities and reviews, two 2-hour slots were booked daily.*

*"Implementing the plan reduced my tours, leaving more time for high-value activities such as planning, reviews, and guidance. I have reduced my weight, my blood pressure level has come down, and my wife is always in a good mood.*

*"I start my day fully energised and am happy the whole day."*

***Sohail, Regional Sales Manager, Dorcas, Marketing Division, Cholayil (Medimix Soap People)***

Who does not want to grow? You, I, all of us want to grow.

And fortunately, we are highly ambitious. We want to grow not only exponentially but also explosively — *bhar-bhar ke*!

The following two routes are available to achieve growth:

1. **The Organic Growth Route:**
   Involves increased output, performance, and efficiency; improved service; reduced costs; expanded customer base; customer retention and repeat orders; fine-tuning the identification, conversion, and customer acquisition processes; brand building; investor confidence; new market and franchise acquisition; new products launch etc.

   The route is controlled in nature, slow in increasing the market share and has a low success rate. But the 'change from within' builds a strong foundation and is self-sustaining.

2. **The Inorganic Growth Route:**
   Involves seeking growth with external help, including from consultants. Exploring new partnerships, joint ventures, mergers, and acquisitions; controlled sale of shares to raise capital; IPOs, and outright sales, are examples of this route.

   Chosen carefully, this route has the potential to ensure rapid and high growth.

The subject matter of this study is limited to the first route, namely, the Organic Route – the growth from within, a change on a long-term and sustained basis.

In an Enterprise, training plays a vital role in developing the Human Capital, directly responsible for driving its growth and providing high value to the Stakeholders For continuous learning, the Human Resource Division draws up elaborate, annual training plans, for employees, at all levels, short and long-term.

The content of most of the training programs consists of two categories: Knowledge and Skills. The processes relating to manufacturing, marketing and sales, service delivery and developing strategies for branding, marketing etc.

Most of this training is conducted in-house; some are outsourced. To minimise the disturbance in the workplace, enterprises focus on short-duration training. For long-term requirements, educational institutions are considered the best source.

Actual use of the learning at the workspace and in the marketplace is expected, but no process exists to ensure tracking of benefits — short or long-term — that the training drive for the trainee, the teams, and the organisation.

The experience shows that only a small number of participants use the learning in an actual work setting and the marketplace— what with the pressure of visits, meetings, MIS, targets, and deadlines. The trainee tends to give low priority to the implementation of the learning. After a week, he can't remember the content of the training. After a month, he can't remember the trainer. After three months, he forgets he ever attended the training.

The training becomes an annual target-driven exercise for the HR Division. Most training/ trainers do not tie up the training output with business results and leave the Human Resource Division with no choice but to focus on the number of training organised and the number nominated.

Moreover, the teaching methodology in all these training – offline or online – is the same: Knowledge and Skills are imparted to the trainees through pedagogy (lectures).

The Born To Win process uses two unique approaches that have not been attempted elsewhere in the training and development arena to address all these issues head-on and to achieve accelerated growth:

1. Use of the Andragogy (Adult) Learning format for conducting the training.
   **Learn from each other by sharing your experiences in a fun, stress-free, non-threatening environment.**

2. Implementation of learning.
   **Not only to get 'results' but 'Delivery against pre-identified measurable goals for the organisation.**

**_Canara Bank Case Study_**

*In the context of rapid growth in the banking sector, increasing competition, dynamic marketplace, and up-gradation of technology, Canara Bank, a Premier Commercial Bank for over 105 years, wished to change the mindset of its Senior Managers to emerge as a Global Bank with Best Practices.*

*Born To Win started with an Attitude Audit of 72 Senior Managers (in 3-groups) – in real-time, at their workplace – in terms of customer experience, response time, ambience, and approachability.*

*The audit identified three areas they needed help:*

*1. Communication – clarity to evoke cooperation.*

*2. Leadership – handle change, mentor teams and take decisions.*

*3. Bridge Differences – manage self and others.*

*Using the Active Experiential Learning format for adults, the Born To Win intervention enabled participants to change their attitudes and behaviours to reach their potential:*

**_Believe, Think and Act as 'Winners'_**

*This self-exploring process helped individuals to discover their personal goals, structure professional goals and align them with the organisation's objectives.*

**_Results_**

*The Managers realised the power of implementation, became more positive, responsible, and accountable; started*

*dealing with change proactively; avoided being judgmental; solutions lie within; focused on listening; better planning and task management to manage stress better.*
*All these brought them more happiness and higher confidence.*

***Feedback***

***D R Chandramathy, Chief Manager:*** *Mobilised retail lending proposals of Rs. 3.60 crores and 251 deposits to meet my targets ahead of the target date.*

***Sudha Venugopal, Manager:*** *Wisdom tool adoption has helped improve my confidence and happiness levels. By not being judgmental, I have been able to ensure better customer service.*

***M N Muralidhara, Chief Manager:*** *The ambience in our branch improved by the contribution of every staff member. Customers noticed and appreciated the change.*

***J S Jagadeesh, Chief Manager:*** *Allotted specific tasks to each employee depending upon their potential. Getting a 'Credit Card' to a customer helped get a considerable deposit.*

# Chapter 3

# The Author, The Organisation

> *"Become more conscious about my work & career. I now positively look at life.*
> *"My self-belief has gone up. I am reading more books to increase my knowledge. Trying a new way of time management, I travel to different work locations in the least time with maximum results.*
> *"I have started thinking about other avenues to increase sales. I have become more receptive to suggestions. I am using quality time on Sundays & holidays to get crucial orders. I advise outstation customers to meet in Delhi during their visits. I advise customers how to place orders from the catalogue etc."*
>
> ***Sandeep Kumar Singh, Senior Territory Sales Manager Luxottica Group***

From childhood, I was taken to writing notes (my journey started with writing with a reed pen, hand-crafted with a knife, dipped in white chalk solution, on a black wooden board) and helping classmates and siblings with their studies. Listening to and telling stories—particularly from Mahabharata—was much fun. The implementation and experimentation with learning intrigued me and became a lifelong passion.

My first job as a lecturer—for a short 6-month tenure—gave me insights into the faculty's role in helping students use classroom learning to pass examinations. Then came the entry into the Indian Customs & Central Excise Service. Right in the beginning (following a gruelling 2-year training period in the classroom and the field), I became aware that the two foundations of

Civil Services—Training and Codification of Processes—could be used effectively to provide adequate service to the citizens.

The focus on training created innumerable opportunities to enhance the performance of the tax officers—at the cutting edge—to enhance taxpayers' experience. I got the chance to experiment with and test different formats of training and exchange ideas—classrooms, group meetings, implementation, self-learning and so on.

Some of my notable experiments were:

- Helping 900 people—the entire population at the Madurai office—to become computer savvy and in a self-learning mode. The process got implemented in a short period, with huge savings. Adopting the new technology became easy, even in a hard-core government environment.

- Digitising the Customs processes for imports and exports in a short period of one month. Training 350 taxmen & importers became the critical factor in the smooth makeover, addressing the initial hiccups.

- The best was the conversion of the Commissioner Appeals' office into a paperless one—a first in a government office. The specialised training of Data Entry Operators helped in accomplishing the project in-house.

By the time I retired as Chief Commissioner, I had become proficient in Adult Learning and Implementation to build effective teams in a tax administration notorious for poor governance. My other strengths were expertise in Change Management; Proficiency in Analysis, Business Process Reengineering, Editorial and Editing Skills, and Thinking on Unstructured Lines. I had a natural flair for Innovation, Troubleshooting, Interpersonal Skills, Conceptualisation and Holistic Approach.

With my "never say die attitude", I was ready to climb the next Mount Everest. I looked for a new profile to give back what I had received to society.

An opportunity arose when during a Rotary meeting, I received an offer to join Leadership Management International, US (LMI) franchise in Chennai. I became a coach to help Senior Managers through the Personal Development programs of LMI. I transformed from a solution provider (as a Tax administrator) to a business coach and trainer exciting, remarkable, and soul-fulfilling.

In LMI, I met Ram Kumarr Seshu, T Ramakrishnan and R Dhirendra. With 60+ Man-years of experience in People Development, this team got together, researched, and conceived the Born To Win process focusing on delivering results through implementation.

The story of Born To Win started with Ram Seshu, the Author of the Born To Win process. Ram, in his earlier stints in the advertising and marketing industry, noticed that even the best performers in the industry failed to get the results they desired. They could not exploit their high potential, leading to frustration and despair. They were usually unhappy and tended to get into a groove (a numbing comfort zone) within five years of starting a job.

A chance conversation with his Gynaecologist made him realise that a child doesn't suffer from any of these inflictions—she is a self-learner, a self-explorer (in the spirit of application), never gives up, never gets bored and is always celebrating and enjoying life.

In 2003, Ram formed an enterprise to launch the process of connecting **'Knowledge & Skills'** through **'Implementation'** to ***'deliver assured results to organisations***. He named it **"Born To Win Learning Services".**

This program was a magnet for me and became my calling: a life mission to help corporations/ institutes improve their bottom line. I joined Born To Win in 2005 and have had the opportunity to deploy the Born To Win process successfully for clients pan India. I am a Director of the Company and Owner of the Delhi franchise.

I have developed as a polymath, excelling in multiple domains. I am a member of the Rotary, Business

Network International (BNI), the Institute of Management Consultants of India and the All India Management Association. I have published papers on Management subjects.

The work culture of the Born To Win family consists of fun, positivity, high energy, with a helping attitude. Continuous interaction and feedback have kept the process dynamic.

The process has, so far, been taken to 2,00,000+ participants from 300+ Organisations, 31+ cities pan India, delivered in 7 languages. The program is top-rated among school and college students, reaching out to 1,00,000+ underprivileged children as part of our pro bono effort.

The program has been implemented in **Manufacturing** (Automotive, Engineering, Pharma and Chemicals, Aviation, Electronics); **Services** (IT, ITES, BPO, Telecom); **Banking** and **Financial Consulting** (SBI, PNB, Canara Bank); **Insurance** (India Insure); **Retail** Reliance Trends, Marks and Spencer); **Food** (Parle, ITC, Godrej); **Apparels** (Arvind); **Power** (ABB, Schneider Electricals); **Hospitals and Healthcare** (TTK); **Real Estate and Construction**; **Hotels and Resorts** (Club Mahindra, GRT Hotels); **Agricultural Business**; **Private Sector** (Large, Medium and Small); **Government Bodies and PSU's** (HAL, BEL); **Government Departments** (India Post, Army) and many more.

**_Toyota Kirloskar Motors Study_**

*Toyota wished to upgrade about 120 Engineers and Officers in the Grade 6 Cadre, from a Learner Level to a Practitioner level. They identified the following set of competencies to be addressed:*

1. *Customer Focus*
2. *Planning and Organising*
3. *Improvement Orientation*
4. *Result Orientation*
5. *Learning and Change Orientation*

**_A Few Feedbacks_**

**_Ratul Sood:_** *I have become more customer-focused. Now there is no time for procrastination at all. I received praise from customers, and I felt happy. My planning has improved, and the results are on time. Stress has come down. I have become more conscious of how I spend time.*

**_Anand:_** *We used the 'Look Beyond the Obvious' learning to analyse the processed and lapsed orders and the stock build-up. The process of PO was altered. We could improve on last year's performance. We made sure that the problem would not arise in future.*

**_Avik:_** *Earlier, our delivery was 75%. We took the target of 80%; we thought we could do it. No such initiative had been taken earlier.*

*We divided the task into 'Bite-Size Chunks'; 'Made Expectations Explicit' for all dealers, and we achieved an 82% success rate.*

*So, we felt great.*

***Rajesh Menon:** For my team, I am now focusing on their strengths and assigning the right job to the right person. 'Attitude of Gratitude' has given me good results with them. I spend 10 minutes with them every day and appreciate them, which I did not do earlier. I saved time and achieved better results in a short span.*

***Arjun:** 'Roadmap', 'Destination' and 'Bite-size Chunks' have helped me a lot, and I could finish my report two days in advance. Earlier, I would do it without planning and then there would be delays. I could help my colleagues with assigned tasks using the' Win-Win' principle. 'Activity Management' has helped me distinguish between Important and Urgent.*

***Vivekananda:** I used planning–time, activity management, and road map led to destination and chalked out a plan to complete tasks pending for six months. My boss has also agreed. I met 20% of those tasks along with regular work, and the process is on. Earlier, a task was given to me, and I would think it wasn't easy, but now when a job is offered, I take it up thinking I CAN and then I plan. My boss also recognised this change after the training.*

***Amol:** There was a problem with scratches on the mirror, recurring for over a year. Our team of 6 people took this issue using the 'Group Dynamics' principle. We found the scratches were due to the packing material. A corrective solution was found, and we felt happy about it.*

# Chapter 4

# The Inspiration

born towin®
learning services pvt. ltd

> *"We already have a dynamic team – of hardworking, talented, skilled individuals. So why would these people now need a personal effectiveness program? But then again, I thought, if I were a successful athlete with a passion for winning and I had an opportunity to compete in a global arena, would I turn them down if someone with a proven track record offered to coach me?*
> *"Thus began our journey with the Born to Win Coaches.*
> *"We were so happy with the changes we experienced in the first group that we offered the program to the rest of the Organisation.*
> *"If I had to summarise the Born to Win process in three words, they would be Simple, Strategic and Successful."*
>
> ***Sudha Panchapakesan, Partner and Head HR, Real Image Media Technologies Pvt. Ltd.***

I was inspired to pen this study as the Born To Win process has affected me positively. I had fallen in love with this new *avatar* as an entrepreneur – to help develop individuals, teams, and organisations to achieve their desired goals, and live happily.

My natural flair for implementation, innovation, interpersonal skills, and holistic approach added to the experience hugely.

The second inspiration came from my experience of the last 17 years working with Born To Win.

I find it disappointing that Enterprises – in the yearly performance reviews – give more importance to the number of training attended than to the benefits of the training accruing to the organisation. Almost no assessments are ever carried out about the **'benefits accruing to the organisation'**, after the training. The question of these benefits being considered **before** selecting the trainee, the training, or the trainer does not even appear on the horizon.

The focus in the training industry also is on imparting Knowledge and Skills. Implementation is taken for granted and not carried out—much less the delivery against pre-identified metrics.

Too bad, the knowledge and learning not implemented don't lead to the results expected by the corporates.

Also, as individuals, as a community and in the corporate world, we take life very seriously. There is no fun, no passion, and no excitement in life. This mindset must change to enjoy whatever we do.

The foremost reason for writing this book is to help organisations fulfil their innermost desire:

*Their sales growth explodes year-on-year, so their bottom line follows a steady growth path.*

Sales team performance is usually a big challenge for all organisations. The teams are expensive to maintain but often get stuck into a rut of self-limiting barriers such as competition, prices, strategy, and slow sales. It is natural but painful.

The Sales teams need to be on the go to deliver against targets—yearly, monthly, and weekly—with confidence, sustained growth, high profitability, improved bottom line, and sustained value to their stakeholders.

The Born To Win process delivers these results in measurable terms. The organisations that have implemented the Born To Win process for their sales team have experienced:

- 30% sales increase in 3 months.
- Closing orders in half the time.
- Repeat Business from the same customers.

*"Born to Win does not teach you anything which is rocket science. It is everyday wisdom; it is common sense – which is not so common. You knew you had to do all those things, but you never did.*

*"The single most significant difference that Born to Win makes is that by practising the Wisdom Tools, you realise, act and enjoy the fruits of the results during the process itself.*

1. *I have felt the need to be more planned in my activities, and using the activity Grid has helped.*
2. *Be more aware of what I say and how I listen, LAER, Explicit expectations etc.*
3. *The team has noticed changes in me–Less reactive, more even-tempered, and more assertive.*

4. *Lifting the team to a new level of excitement has made me happy.*
5. *Focus on personal health, including giving up on cigarettes, has made me happy."*

**Bala Raman, CEO, *Congruent Solutions***

# Chapter 5

## The Child - The Natural Winner

born towin®
learning services pvt. ltd

*"I don't get upset on every comment – stop being judgmental. I have stopped cribbing about things not achieved. This has helped me in doing the tasks positively.*
*"I have also become aware of my capabilities. I get time for myself at the end of the day.*
*"I have started listening to my team and sharing their lives.*
*"I have started issuing cases personally to the Engineers – one person responsible for one case for easy manageability. I make my expectation explicit. This has improved their involvement and tracking of the cases. We manage better by planning. Most jobs/ cases were completed on time or ahead of time. The number of cases handled by each Engineer has increased."*

***Kiranpreeth Singh, Sr. Project Engineer, ICAT***

What are the Winning Attitudes and Behaviours of a Child that inspired Ram to write the winning Born To Win process and that we need to emulate to bring zing to our life?

**And why is the child a born winner?**

**She is a self-learner:** She learns to communicate independently; the adults provide the language. She knows to walk on her own; she neither looks for encouragement nor is worried about the outcome.

**She is always happy:** Never sad for long, bubbling with energy and showing it. Laughter is natural to her, with or without any reason. Doesn't seek attention or approval all the time. Never worry about right or wrong.

**She is curious:** Cool, super observant and persistent. Always positive, disregarding temporary incidents, accidents, and obstacles. Is not afraid of taking risks; doing things differently is natural. She learns from her mistakes. That's how civilisation has made progress.

**Starts the journey of life and goes through it with a sense of bewilderment.**

**She believes everyone, easily:** Human beings, and even animals. Share with others (help others) by giving them choices.

**She never gives up**: Never gives up on failure(s) or challenge(s). Keeps going till she gets what she fancies. Keep exploring and keep-at-it, never ever getting bored. Success, failures, happiness, disappointments—all are taken along.

**She is not afraid to ask for help:** Cries for assistance in meeting her basic needs—food and hygiene.

**She operates from the Win-Win paradigm** (against Win-Lose): Never worries about the opinion or comments of others. She is comfortable with and enjoys her life journey through her baby steps (bite-size chunks) to achieve whatever she fancies.

The Born To Win process promises to bring out the 'Child Within', her Enthusiasm, Bewilderment, Positivity, and Joy of Life.

> *"To rekindle what has been forgotten along the way… that all of us are Born Winners"*, to serve humanity.

Mahatma Gandhi recognised:

> *"If we can bridge the gap between what we do and what we are capable of doing, we would never step back from any opportunity put forward to us."*

And so did Swami Vivekananda when he reiterated the Winning Attitude of the child:

> *"All the powers in the universe are already ours. It is we who have put our hands before our eyes and cry that it is dark."*

***The Born To Win process has been designed for Indian culture and ethos, using Indian case studies bereft of jargon.***

"A structured emotional motivation to move forward. We saw clarity in our 3- and 6 months goals after two weeks of the Born To Win process.

"We ran the Born to Win process through our senior team, and then it caught on like fire. The alignment of Attitude and Approach across the organisation has taken place.

"The following results were caused by the ignition provided by Born to Win:

"Over 4 months: In 5 Divisions, the Quality improved from 7% to 58% and the Productivity from 17% to 87%.

"Over 15 months: In the 5 Divisions, the Quality improved from 73% to 97% and the Productivity from 31% to 181%.

"We have, therefore, committed that all our 2000 people will be exposed to one or the other program of Born To Win.

"Enhanced Time-Productivity: Got to spend two weekends with family in January."

***P Mukund, MD, Igarishi Motors***

# Chapter 6

# *The Process That Delivers*

> *"Born to Win was a very new kind of an experience for me – it was the first time I had attended a process like this.*
> *"It lets you think about your creative energy, which is very different from any other training program.*
> *"On an organisational level regarding KrishCricket and my people, it was of great help. Since it ensures consistent implementation of the learning, it is successful."*
>
> ***'Kris' Srikkanth, MD, Kriscricket.com, (the then Chairman, Indian Selection Committee)***

The Born To Win process was written after 3-year research. The analysis revealed three broad attitude issues about why young adults fail to operate to their full potential:

1. Low self-confidence.
2. Fear of Failure.
3. Inability to focus on Priorities (the big picture).

At the workplace, these attitudes manifest themselves as:

| | |
|---|---|
| **Lack of Self Confidence** | • Inability to make decisions.<br>• Inability to manage change.<br>• Inability to work in a team.<br>• Inability to handle pressure. |
| **Fear of Failure** | • Operate from a comfort zone.<br>• Escalation of problems.<br>• Lack of Asking Effective Questions.<br>• Reluctance to reinvent. |
| **Inability to Focus on Priorities** | • Inefficient work habits.<br>• Taking a myopic view of tasks.<br>• Inability to grow. |

Performance Improvement: Working on the Existing Potential

Better ROI

Performance Enhancement: Develop and Use More of the Hidden Potential

*The Born To Win process not only addresses all these issues but also acts as a catalyst for growth and development. The life-changing experience of positive work culture makes it growth-oriented.*

*A robust belief system nurtures professionals' behavioural patterns to help them produce optimum results on a self-sustaining basis.*

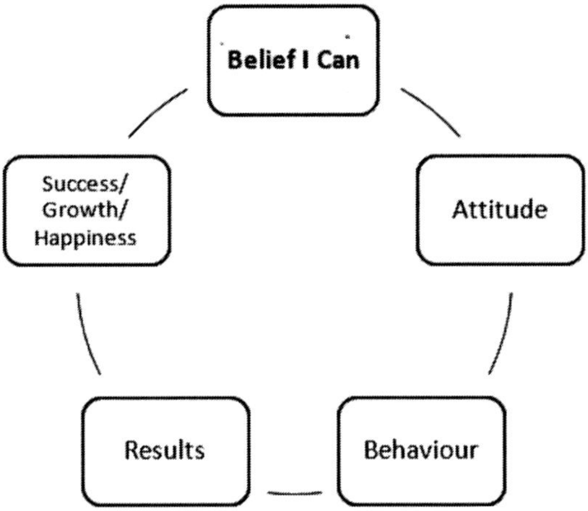


Our Attitudes (habit of thought) lead to Behaviours (habit of action), which in turn lead to Results. The results that are positive for you are Success for you. Success leads to Development/ Growth and finally to Happiness. It is the happiness that reinforces our Self-belief. Self-belief provides us with the confidence/attitude for action—supporting our Self-motivation.

The objective is to help an individual "Believe, Think and Act as a Winner". In other words: "If I Can't, Then Who Else Can."

The Born To Win is a multi-layered people transformation process that awakens you to your full potential. It bridges the gap between what people know and what people do.

Self-belief connects you with nourishing aspects of Indian culture and traditions and looks at Universal Truths: Human Values, Integrity, non-judgmental, Positivity, Humility, and Spirituality.

Once you start getting results for yourself, you have the confidence to take it to your team and, from there, to the organisation, leading to sustained growth.

Not surprisingly, Born To Win has no competitors in the marketplace.

***Finally, Born To Win proves that it is not merely hard work that gets us the desired results—we need the right attitude and smart work.***

*"'Think I Can' helped me to be in high morale. Using the Win-Win principle, I could channel team members' strengths to deliver better. Made my expectations explicit to the team. Earlier I had to follow up 5-6 times. Now I am doing it once or twice. Productivity has increased.*

*"Earlier, some of my personal tasks would not get done. Activity Management helped me to prioritise my task and get more clarity. Once it is listed in the grid, it is difficult to ignore.*

*"I am using 'pattern' to be positive in taking the urgent decisions on projects, make accurate analysis and work with a very high self-esteem."*

***Neeraj Kumar Singh, Team Lead, ITC Infotech***

# Chapter 7

# The Two Missing Pieces in Corporate Training

*"I think positively about issues that were reasons for anger. I look for other ways of solving problems. I have learned how to make life simpler, better and result oriented.*
*"All my carpool partners have noticed that I have started enjoying traffic jams – I use that time for planning. I prepare a plan on the Management Grid and then change the routine.*
*"I told my team I wanted SAP to be implemented by Sep 1, 2010, and we succeeded."*

***Rakesh Garg, Accounts Officer, ICAT***

The uniqueness of the Born To Win process is its focus on the 'delivery on assured results'. To achieve the effectiveness of the delivery, the process stands on two pillars.

**1. Adult Learning**

The Born To Win process uses the Adult Learning format for its delivery.

All corporate training is conducted for 'adults', but the format used for their delivery is 'Pedagogy' (child learning). The knowledge and skills are brought to the trainee from outside through lecturing and preaching.

And lecturing is one format we all adults dislike.

The slate of an adult is written, cleaned-in full, or partially, overwritten, several times over. This is what experience is about – a collection of successes, mistakes and failures.

The adult tends to check all inputs against this experience. He develops a desire to explore the world on his terms, beyond the world of his parents and teachers. He has moved forward in life.

Adult Learning involves "ask and encourage"; rather than "tell and expect" in the case of Child Learning.

The Born To Win process uses this Adult or Experiential Learning format (Andragogy) that respects young minds.

There are three essential principles of Adult Learning:

i. Adult learning takes place by sharing experiences with co-participants.

   That is why the Born To Win process is conducted in groups of 20-25 participants who share their experiences and arrive at learning from within the group.

   Learned from within, it becomes 'My Learning'.

ii. Adults learn best when the environment for learning is a non-threatening one.

   The environment in the Born To Win sessions is stress-free, fun-filled, and easy-going. The sharing of experiences becomes interactive, engaging and highly exploratory. It encourages a free flow of thoughts and ideas that enrich the whole group—keeping 'hidden agenda' and 'stress' out. No pompous jargon: the environment is that of success and exhilaration.

iii. An adult learns only when he sees the results for himself.

Starting with the first session, the participant starts seeing the results he and other group members obtained. By the end of the program, the participant is implementing the learning on his goals and getting results again and again.

He has internalised the process of doing **More, Better and Faster**.

Several benefits flow from the use of the Experiential Learning Format:

i. Sharing experiences/ thoughts is natural to an adult—she wants to test her knowledge, remove her doubts, validate her views, and get clarity on her thought process to accept a new concept/ subject.

   In the environment of pedagogy, this tendency of an adult is stifled, leading to the in-built resistance of an adult.

ii. **The format provides the building block, the first step towards delivery against the agreed-upon goals**:

'My Learning' converts to 'Ownership' to get him 'Excited' for its 'Implementation'. Recall your excitement after acquiring a new mobile—you spent long hours learning all the features that very evening itself.

This excitement brings enthusiasm to work on 'My Goals' (work-related and personal) with passion.

Achievement of success becomes easier to visualise, and this visualisation provides 'Self-motivation'.

Repeated, the concepts of 'My Learning', 'My Implementation', 'Ownership', 'My Goals', 'My Motivation, and 'My Results' get internalised.

His 'Self-Confidence' aka 'I Can Quotient' goes up.

iii. **The experience-sharing format makes it easier to build a great team**:

The sharing builds on effective communication and bonding.

Be non-judgmental: "I may not agree with your views, but you can't be wrong as you are also talking based on your experiences."

Sharing helps overcome the biggest challenge of not listening to each other at work.

The resultant healthy group dynamics build on the **culture of trust** in the team and people around. The trust builds on the team's confidence to generate new ideas, take risks, and take responsibility for achieving 'Organisational Goals'.

The participant also understands that the solutions lie within; the power of thinking differently, managing yourself and your resources and understanding and acquiring 'ownership'.

The culture of fun, joy and togetherness prevails at the workplace – going beyond the trap of 'doing a job.

**2. Implementation**

The second pillar that delivers assured results is the focus on Implementation.

Only when you implement do you come to know whether the learning – you have had in the Adult Learning format – works for you or not. That too in real-time situations. This would also apply to your knowledge and skills.

The first step for implementation is writing down your goal and an action plan. Writing it down makes you commit to action, disregarding all excuses, taking you out of your comfort zone and motivating you.

Three situations would arise when you start Implementing:

i. **You are successful**
   Success excites you and provides the motivation for repeating the implementation process – 'Self-motivation' is enhanced and sustained, strengthening your **attitudes and behaviours**.

ii. **You fail**
   Creates an opportunity to try differently, with 'different action'. A chance to overcome:

*"If you continue to do the same thing the same way, you'll continue to get the same results."*

Your thought process will change if the 'different action' gets you the desired results. You have taken a step in **transforming your attitude and changing your mindset**.

Coming from within, acceptance of the change would be easier and will strengthen your confidence, to try again and again.

By acting differently, you have **enhanced your risk-taking capacity.**

Moreover, by taking challenges as opportunities, you accept 'failures' and 'mistakes' as part of your success journey.

iii. **You did not implement**

The spaced process encourages you to try again and again – until you get comfortable with the implementation process.

This addresses the 'feeling of guilt' or 'shame' that emerges from procrastination, not trying. The focus shifts to persistence until the implementation process is no longer challenging.

***'My Learning'*** *and* ***'My Implementation' connect*** *to* ***'My Goal'. More practice*** *will lead to* ***measurable results*** *on* ***'My Desirable Goal'*** *on a* ***sustained basis.***

It is like swimming. Reading a book on swimming, watching swimmers, or watching their videos will not make you a swimmer. You'll have to get into the water (implementation), take some dips, swallow some water (overcome challenges and failures), and persist as a swimmer. Eventually, you enjoy your mastery over water.

The process is not against planning *per se* but complements the conventional focus on strategy.

The first stage of Implementation is planning. At this stage, you sit down to define your goal, the resources available to you (including staffing requirements) and the time frame. The Born To Win process encourages planning – ***one hour invested in planning saves three in implementation***.

In the modern-day corporate world, much importance is given to strategy, purely a theoretical exercise. Different models are prepared after investing a lot of time and energy, with little realising eventually, these models will have to be tested through implementation.

That is why the Born To Win process recommends getting into execution at the earliest. Prepare a workable plan, identify three easy-to-implement ideas and start with one—making changes as one goes along.

Within each team, each idea would be subdivided into smaller easy-to-implement tasks for working by individuals to ensure timely achievement. Agility becomes a password for quick execution.

Deploy more teams to make the process faster.

The motivation of the team will go up as each part is completed. 'Celebration' of success plays an important role. The passion provides the impetus for completing the project—efficiently and faster—making the entire experience enjoyable.

Perhaps, a mix of the two would work out best: the 80:20 formula— strategizing being given lesser time and importance.

The implementation helps the participant to –

- Internalise the process of getting the desired results, translating his ambition into action.
- Start Managing Self, his Work and the People around him.
- Manage the ever-lengthening list of pending tasks.
- Find innovative solutions for his pain points.
- Achieve Work-Life balance.
- Addresses high stress and anxiety in day-to-day life.
- Have fun, enjoy whatever he does and start leading a satisfying life.

***The Implementation has made the Born To Win process a 'Life-Changing Experience'.***

*"I am approaching people to improve my team participation, Time Management and Attitude. Fear of failure has gone – no fear of taking new initiatives. I have improved Customer satisfaction with follow-up calls. 86% target achieved in acquiring new customers by making my destination clear.*
*"My focus is now on Customers' promotion. I currently make sure to have much fun in monthly review meetings.*
*"I decide whether I will be happy or not at the beginning of the day."*

***Raghavendra Hegde, Inside Sales Lead, Microsoft***

# Chapter 8

# The Magical Course - Content

born towin®
learning services pvt. ltd

*"Earlier, we worked in different directions; now, we work in synergy. All departments know their responsibilities, and the reports go on time.*

*"By improving the Planning Structure, we have achieved an efficiency of 97% in our dispatches against a target of 96%.*

*"On the personal front, my confidence level has gone up. Planning has improved, and so has time-bound execution. I have been able to improve communication by interacting both with internal and external customers.*

*"I have now become more time conscious: I give more time to my family and have improved my social life. This makes me happy."*

***Puneet Banga, Factory Manager, International Flavours and Fragrances, India***

The course content of this result-oriented process is a holistic one, too:

- Achieve Work-Life Balance in all six areas of life: *Career, Health, Family, Lifelong-Learning, Sports-Hobby and Social-Spiritual. This has acquired much focus in these difficult times.*

- In practice, it translates into Self-management: *Managing sleep, exercise, nutrition, leisure, time and stress; and managing change and technology. It is also the management of group dynamics to help achieve organisational goals.*

- Bridge the gap between knowledge and results by focusing on Implementation that is conducive to self-exploration.

- Do everything with passion, and enjoy life's journey.

The process is a Positive Life-changing experience to create happy and result-oriented work culture; to address some of the critical issues that lead to Inefficient Action:

- Getting into your comfort zone.
- Non-alignment with organisational vision.
- Low self-belief in themselves and the team.
- Not communicating with clarity for results.
- Constant firefighting.
- Living a reactive life, full of stress.
- Not listening to the customer.
- Not developing an internal customer mindset.

To achieve all this, one has to operate from high Self-Belief. Go that extra mile to rise above the ordinary because I know 'I CAN'.
The process is based on the philosophy that –

***A robust Belief system creates a positive attitude and behavioural pattern in individuals and teams, enabling them to unleash their full potential, achieve their goals and produce optimum results.***

The Born To Win is the process of Conditioning Continuum.

Conditioning inputs start very early and last throughout a lifetime. These inputs impact the thought process. Thoughts determine actions which in turn are reflected in results.

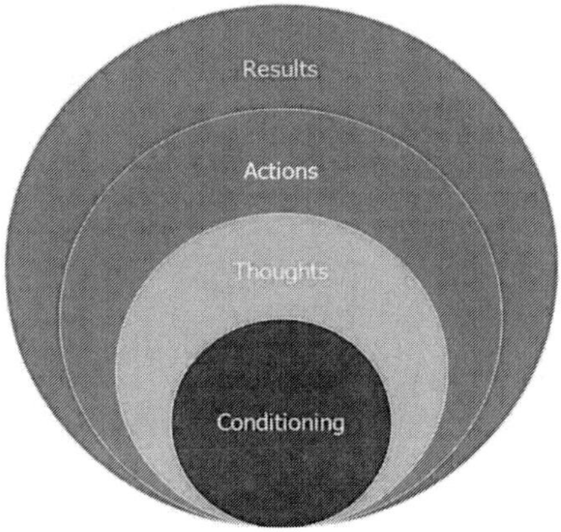


Conscious adoption of enabling thoughts will result in positive actions that lead to desired results.

**Sessions Structure**

**Session 1 – Believe I Can**
**Topics Covered:**

- Importance of being an 'I CAN' Person.
- Why does the process deliver what it promises?

**Deliverables, Participants Appreciate:**

- The 'I CAN' attitude will serve them best to enhance their motivation.
- It is essential to participate fully in an exciting process that is oriented toward desired results.

**Session 2—Who Am I (Discovering & Managing Self)**

**Topics Covered:**

- Self-evaluation of strengths, weaknesses, attitudes, behaviours, and values.
- Culture worksheet of the organisation.

**Deliverables, Participants Appreciate:**

- The Understanding Culture of the organisation—What the organisation means to me and how my strengths fit in with my organisation's needs.
- Building a roadmap leading to the organisation's desired destination.
- Importance of developing a proactive approach towards organisational change and the market.

**Session 3—How I Can Work SMART**

**Topics Covered:**

- Managing Activities.
- SMART goals.

**Deliverables, Participants Appreciate:**

- Manage tasks, not time to minimise stress and anxiety. Prioritise them in urgent, essential and imperative categories to achieve them quickly.
- The benefits of taking time out for planning.
- Delegation is essential to growing an organisation *exponentially.*

- Identifying opportunities that yield good results.
- Setting goals—both in their work and personal life—that are SMART and result-oriented and achieve Work-Life balance.

**Session 4—How do I Work with Others**

**Topics Covered:**

- Group Dynamics.
- Effective Communication—Expectations, Team Building.

**Deliverables, Participants Appreciate:**

- A comprehensive idea of how to work with others in a team, get teams to work for them, delegate, motivate, and empathise with team members.
- How to consistently meet internal and external expectations to build a great team.
- Learning to make your Communication Effective—how to Speak, how to Listen and how to say NO.

**Session 5— How do I Sustain I Can**

**Topics Covered:**

- Self-Image—the key to a confident 'I'.
- Overcoming the Fear of Failure.
- Wisdom working.

**Deliverables, Participants Appreciate:**

- How Self-worth contributes in considerable measure to their Self-confidence.
- An easy-to-implement method to overcome Fear of Failure.

- The principles of Wisdom Working: The key to building excellent WIN-WIN relationships.

**Final Session 6— Disciplining I Can**

**Topics Covered:**

- Recap of learning they had from the program.
- The participants and the teams share the learning they have used, where and the results they obtained.

**Deliverables, Participants Appreciate:**

- Share their experiences and results with the whole group.
- Become aware of the goals they achieved for the Organisation (identified beforehand).
- They commit to implementing the learning in their day-to-day lives for the rest of their lives.
- The impactful process helps to Manage Self, Manage Work and Manage People—

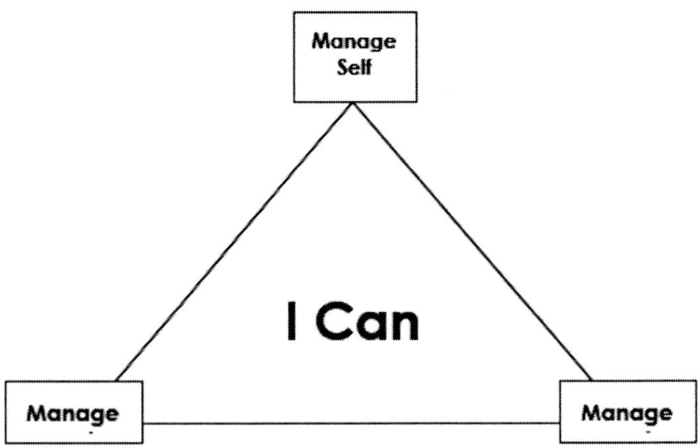

Thereby enhancing the **'I Can' Quotient**—to do things **More, Faster and Better.**

This Self-Introspective process helps individuals to discover their **Personal Goals,** structure **Professional Goals** and align them with **Organisational Goals**.

***Finally, it helps the individual to manage the ecosystem and lead a life of fulfilment.***

*"All 26 participants are now on the same page, in sync.*
*"The team is transformed – non-performing members have become performers. I find more energy from fewer resources.*
*"In several parameters such as Acquisitions, Cost Optimisation and Client Churn Rate Reduction, the progress has been so drastic that HQ has started referring to UP East as a benchmark to other Circles. Earlier, our ratings were not high among different regions in the country.*
*"Some participants started exercising daily. One reduced his weight from 94 to 88 kg.*
*"Most of them started giving more time to their families."*

***Vikash Choubey, Head HR, TATA Teleservices (Regional Sales Team)***

# Chapter 9

## *The Benefits*

***Bimal Maruti Agency*** *(24 outlets all over Bangalore)*

***Objective***

*Think of practical solutions that can be implemented at the workplace to:*

1. *Foster coordination and cooperation among the team members.*
2. *Remove hurdles to ensure a free communication flow to enhance overall effectiveness.*

***Feedback***

***A Thangaraj****: More focused on what is required: Urgent–Important–Not important. Accordingly, everyday activities were streamlined. More responsibility has been shared with the second-line team members. There is a decrease in customer complaints. I am looking forward to overall dealership growth.*

***Tanuja M S:*** *I have noticed many changes in myself either in my personal or professional life, by taking the initiative and much involvement in work: Punctuality, Responsibility, Honouring commitments, and Daily planning. SMART Goals: Working according to the promise.*

***Anil Kumar L****: This program made me analyse everything, handle all my weaknesses and bring solutions to all the problems. I have started admitting my mistakes. All customer commitments are honoured, and they were satisfied. I am celebrating every success along with the team.*

There are several benefits of the 'Life Changing' Born To Win experience:

1. Working on achieving goals brings ownership, pride, responsibility, commitment and accountability. The empowered team finally drives the organisation's desired results (Growth and Development).

   **'I Can'** becomes **'We Can'** to drive the results for the organisation.

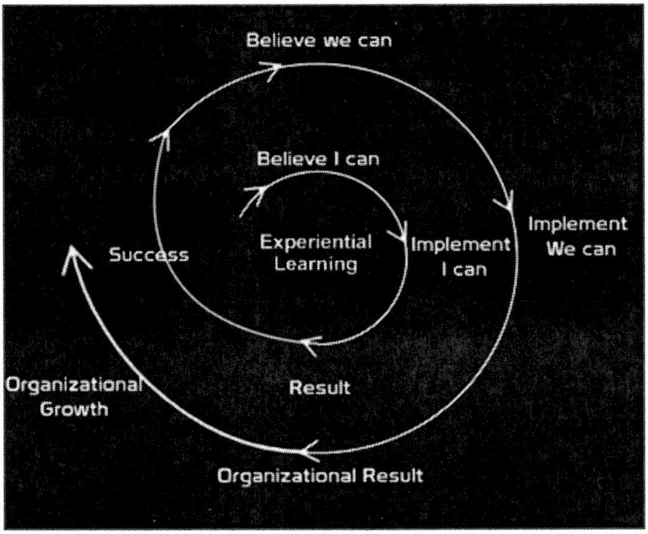


2. Look at and align with the big picture, to define his goals, and achieve big. Also, to understand life's purpose.
3. 'Simple' yet 'Powerful' approach of 'Self-exploration' focuses on issues to awaken the potential of each participant.

4. The 'Experiential Learning' format helps the participant to transcend the mundane level and operate from an 'I Can' level.
5. Focus on 'Implementation' in real-time situations rather than 'Knowledge and Skills' or 'Strategy' to reach his goals quickly and easily. It translates the participant's high ambition into action to achieve his dreams.
6. 'Repetition' of the process week after week leads to internalisation of the process of Delivery of Results.
7. The goals keep changing with the ever-changing environment. Focus on the process develops detachment from the goals to connect with their spirituality.
8. Identify what is holding him back, to find a solution within, with the confidence of 'I Can'. Find innovative solutions for his pain points and fears too.
9. Be proactive in dealing with the change in customers' expectations—both external and internal.

**Time Management**

1. Schedule time for things Important for him (high-payoff activities) and relaxation. The relaxation becomes a period of reflection and inspiration—to sharpen the axe.
2. Focus on easy-to-implement ideas in baby steps to build momentum and motivation. Avoid getting overwhelmed by multi-tasking and save time.

3. Plan and prioritise the ever-lengthening list of pending tasks to avoid stress.
4. Track his progress regularly—at his own pace, time, and place—to achieve his goals efficiently and quickly; and sustain Self-confidence.
5. Keep 'delegating'—to man and machine—to keep the organisation technology-driven and agile and find time for higher priority tasks.
6. Crises can't be anticipated or prevented, but one can prepare for them.
7. Work on his 'Work-Life' balance to lead a purposeful life. Reach in time and leave on time.

**Team Building**

1. Start with **'What can I do more to complete the task?'** and go to **'What can we do more to complete the task?'** The game of 'taking credit' gets thrown out of the window.
2. From a Human Capital perspective, the question is how to get teams to work seamlessly and deliver enhanced performance against the Pre-Specified goals.
3. Getting sustained results becomes a norm, not an exception—for the individual, the teams, and the organisation.
4. Work on group dynamics to build productive teams.
5. The experience-sharing format provides a platform for 'Communication'—at different

levels—the opportunity to think, write and express in a non-threatening environment.

6. Effective communication is the responsibility of the speaker, not of the listener.
7. Listen before reacting. Write to crystallise thoughts to communicate effectively.
8. Active listening is the key to building trust.
9. Collaborate to develop commitment for making functional teams effective to implement together.
10. Empathy and making expectations explicit are the two building blocks to building an effective team.

**Attitudes and Behaviours**

1. Self-Belief builds belief in others to enhance performance together.
2. Create a positive work culture to help others to sustain growth.
3. Work on stretch and action-oriented goals; to challenge yourself to keep your motivation high and overcome the fear of failure.
4. Managing change is about dealing with change proactively.
5. To maintain happiness levels, stay away from perfectionism.
6. Accept life as it comes, have no regrets over the past, no anxiety for the future— Be Positive.
7. Take control of your life's remote. Enjoy whatever you do, keep learning—bring FUN

back into your life to reduce high stress and anxiety levels.

8. Be more comfortable with yourself and accept all warts and blemishes. If you accept yourself, the whole world will be with you.
9. Work on your own and each others' strengths to build a happy organisation.
10. Reward yourself for the little wins and celebrate the big ones to maintain your motivation level high. Lead a satisfying life; be content.
11. Operate from the Win-Win paradigm (against Win-Lose) to be positive to grow exponentially.
12. Explore your hidden potential.
13. Connect with the nourishing aspects of your 'Values' and 'Traditions'.

**Build on Your Risk-Taking Capacity**

1. Develop an innovative attitude – do things differently to build risk-taking capacity.
2. Keep reinventing yourself through attitudinal and behavioural change, taking growth to the next level, and adapting to the ever-changing world.
3. Come out of your comfort zone continuously to challenge yourself and make progress.
4. The main task of an effective leader is to provide a vision of the future, and a plan for achieving it, modify the project as per needs

and move forward fearlessly—accept failure as part of the journey.

> *"Born to Win is a timely intervention to bring 'positivity' to the minds of Team Leaders and General Managers.*
> *"The best part of the program has been the coming together of the senior people who do not find time to discuss much in an 'open' atmosphere to understand each other in a much better manner. Open communication has brought about positivity in the peer group. In customer initiatives, by being non-value judgmental and speaking with empathy, the problems are understood in a better perspective to resolve collectively."*
>
> ***R Rajakumar, General Manager, Hyundai Motors India Ltd.***

# Chapter 10

# The Structure

*"Born to Win is an innovative Organization with an 'Alternative' approach to making ordinary people realise their Extraordinary potential. A unique, exciting and most importantly, flexible program makes it an asset for managing and motivating large teams.*

*"I am seeing remarkable changes in the participants' attitude: Improved commitment; sincerity; ownership; anger management; appreciation of point of view of others; less argumentative, positive attitude. The participants are proud of the value they can add to the organisation after the intervention.*

*"On a personal level, I find it easier to pull myself out of a low phase – bad day/ meeting – into a positive mood. My friends and I find me more relaxed and outgoing and less complaining."*

***Nupur Sood, Assistant VP, Citibank Collection Centre***

The Born To Win process that delivers assured results against pre-identified metrics is spread over several stages:

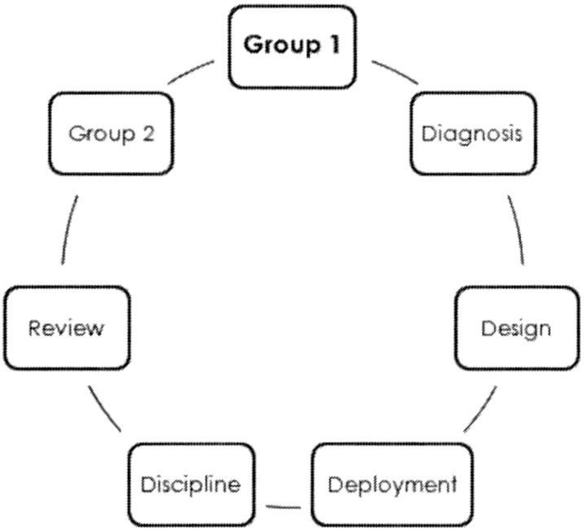

1. **Diagnosis:**
   - Interact with Senior Management and Operational Heads to understand specific issues and drivers of growth and arrive at the particular metrics for delivery.
   - Identify the sales team (up to 25 people) that will be taken through the process.

2. **Design:**
   - Customise the process to suit the deliverable metrics.

3. **Deployment:**
   - Deploy the highly Interactive and Exploratory approach that encourages the free flow of thoughts and ideas, which helps understand the benefit of learning from others.
   - The experiential learning format, conducted in a fun, non-threatening atmosphere, addresses conditioning issues that ensure the delivery of desired results.
   - Six weekly sessions last for 4-hours each.
   - Icebreakers, pointers, games, and situational analysis are used in the sessions to engage participants in a learning experience that is not preachy.
   - Each group is mentored by a facilitator who initiates and maintains an open and lively dialogue.
   - It makes them realise solutions lie within, understand the power of thinking differently,

group dynamics, how to manage themselves and their resources, and take charge of the life.

4. **Discipline:**

- Each week, the individual sets five goals—2 goals work related, 1-team and 2-personal.
- Each session ends with a recap of the learning and how the participant would apply them to his goals.
- In between the sessions, a participant works on his and the team's goals—using the concept of baby steps. He is encouraged to work from his strength's perspective and with positivity.
- During the intervening days, he receives motivational emails.
- The next session begins by reviewing the learning of the previous session and sharing how their application helped a participant work on his goals. These reviews, by sharing results, are highly motivating and enhance bonding.
- In the sixth session, all the participants share the results they got. They become aware of the results they achieved for the organisation—against the pre-identified deliverable metrics. They also appreciate the focus on 'why' and 'how', not 'what'.

5. **Review:**

- To stay the course, the participant's track progress on their individual and team goals, week on week.

- Their progress is also captured in the mid and last sessions.
- A Review meeting after a 45-day gap ensures the sustainability of the process.
- The facilitator submits a performance report of the Group to the management and starts the process for the next group.

**Bonus:**

Carry out a high-valued 'Attitude Audit' to help identify the goals—at the individual, team, and organisational levels.

*All these stages have evolved dynamically over the last 19 years of our proven track record. These are designed to provide high value to individuals, teams and organisations and achieve desirable and sustainable results in measurable terms.*

*"I had thought that my job responsibility was to treat and take care of the sick, but after attending the Born To Win session, I realised that I have a greater responsibility in the productivity of the company.*
*"I know the contribution I must make and how to move forward."*

***Dr. T B Sailesh, Medical Officer, Wabco***

# Chapter 11

## The Winning Game

### *Mainetti Group*

***Objective***

1. *Successful Inter-Departmental Coordination.*
2. *Improved Organisational Structure (Skills, Systems, People, Infrastructure).*
3. *Achieve Customer Delight: Move from 5/10 to 9.5/10 (Quality, Faster Service Compliance, On-time Delivery, Responsiveness, Value for Money).*

***Outcome***

*The Team was set up to improve Interdepartmental Coordination focused on Stores and Logistics coordination. A new storage system was designed, FIFO was introduced, damage to the stocks was reduced, and new stickers with barcodes were intended to minimise wrong dispatches. Consequently, the Sales Dept. could reduce the non-moving inventories by 5-7%.*

*The Team set up for improving the Organisational Structure could help the Finance Dept. to reduce their outstanding by Rs. 80 lakhs and enhance the cash flow by Rs. 100 lakhs. Also, workforce Planning Data was made available to Admin. Dept. in advance.*

*In the Sales Dept. (the Inter-Departmental Coordination), they could hold two meetings of all departments; views shared; better appreciation of each other's difficulties; teacups changed; parking of vehicles in front to the gate improved; water availability improved; focus on customer delight.*

***Highlights***

*Initially, in the group activities in the Born To Win sessions, the seniors used to dictate their views on the entire group. By*

*the third session, the seniors started listening, and the group interaction improved.*
*The Sales Team started appreciating the constraints of the Production Team. The Production Team stopped living in isolation and started keeping the latter informed of their challenges. They stopped 'judging' each other. Both realised they were serving the Customer.*
*The Finance Team was amazed that they started getting information from other Depts. on time. They could complete and submit to the Board their MIS reports ahead of time. All they did was to 'Make their Expectations Explicit' – explaining their requirements precisely and in advance to other departments.*
*The practice of writing and sharing helped them to express their views frankly to the seniors, overcoming the fear of public speaking. One of the lady participants admitted that she was no more afraid of interacting with her male supervisors or seniors from anywhere in the organisation 'unchaperoned'.*
*The entire group was proud of the results they had achieved in the duration of the process (5 weeks). That the Senior Management was not present while sharing the program's outcome did not put them off.*
*The choice of Inter-departmental coordination as their first organisational goal indicated awareness of their weaknesses and preparedness to work on them. They also realised that coordination was critical for individual, departmental and organisational growth.*

The organisations that have implemented the Born To Win process for their sales team have experienced:

- 30% sales increase in 3 months.
- Closing orders in half the time.
- Repeat Business.

The results are measurable, assured and sustaining as the **Sales Team** acquires 'Ownership' of the team, the Organisation, and the entire workplace. It gets the conviction: **Implementation of the learning is a fun activity and the key to success**—on their goals, at their own pace. Becomes convinced tracking increases the visibility of their progress and is, therefore, self-motivating. Internalises the process of getting results and celebrating success, thereby sustaining it.

Importantly, acquiring learning through sharing experiences is easily acceptable and everlasting.

At the individual level, the program helps you to enhance your **I CAN Quotient**, taking your belief level to 10X. You take over responsibility for implementation and results—to change your 'Attitudes and Behaviours' to achieve 'success'—and become proactive in dealing with Change. By learning the art of managing 'Self', 'Goals' and 'People around', you take over accountability for your assigned tasks and actions.

***Bring passion into life and enjoy whatever you do.***
Be 'Positive'—learn from the past; the future doesn't exist—and accept the present to contain anxiety and stress. Also, taking failures as part of your 'life journey';

builds on your risk-taking capacity. You learn to be gentle with who you are and operate from high 'Self-Esteem' to be a winner forever.

Finally, you start operating from the 'Win-Win' paradigm. **If I make my team Win, my Win is automatic**.

*"I have tried win-win in Price Negotiation Committee meetings with the vendors – both in subcontracting and equipment purchases. This has resulted in savings.*
*"In projects, 'I Can' is essential. By empowering people, new ideas are implemented in every area – civil works or services – resulting in satisfaction.*
*"Proactive intervention with the customers resulted in orders in AL31FP and RD33 Series III."*

***V. Balakrishnan, Assistant General Manager, HAL***

# Chapter 12

# The Two Choices

> *"The results after the training program were terrific.*
> *"Our second line team is charged up and has started involving themselves in the growth of self and company. They have become more positive and have learned to grow confidence in their decision-making. They have also become more accountable for their work.*
> *"The money spent on them is more than recovered in just a matter of 1 month. All further benefits are profit."*
>
> ***Sunil Baglani, CEO, Neri Engineering***

With this picture on the horizon, you have two options to choose from:

**Choice 1**
Continue to do what you have been doing, the way you have been doing and continue to get the same results.

**Choice 2**
Allow us to come in as a partner in your business growth to -

- Understand your business and your pain points related to the performance of your sales team.
- Share with you how we can transform your sales team into a high-performing asset—in measurable terms, on a sustained basis—week after week, month after month, year after year.
- Identify the group of salespersons to initiate the process.
- Identify the deliverable metrics for the group.
- Start the Born To Win process.

- Deliver the assured results in 90 days.
- Continue the process with the next group.

For the growth of any enterprise—corporate, industry, organisation, institute, in the public or private sector—continuous training of human capital is imperative. In the current market scenario, without any exception—all training programs offer Knowledge & Skill training.

*And, these offerings do not address the real issues of Attitude Transformation and Mindset Change.*

Born To Win does not impart training, we help participants & teams to internalise the process of getting results—consistently & on a sustained basis.

Contact Anand Chhabra: +91 98718 55829; anandchhabra@borntowin.co.in

# Annexure

born towin®
learning services pvt. ltd

# Results Delivered In Other Functional Areas

Born To Win works with your key people to achieve measurable results per pre-specified targets, which are crucial to your organisation.

1. **Performance Enhancement**
    - Improve Profitability through Increased Sales; Reduce Wastage and Costs in a Short Duration.
    - Enhance Productivity, Quality, On-time Delivery and Customer Satisfaction.
    - Develop a Creative, Innovative mindset to Do Things Differently; Build Risk Taking Capacity.

2. **Human Capital Quality Enhancement**
    - Planned, Organised, and Disciplined Action.
    - Enhanced Efficiency and Quality of Work Life.
    - Fewer Accidents; Grievances; Lower Absenteeism, Churn Rate.
    - Be Relaxed in the Workplace and Provide Service with a Smile.
    - Create a culture of Happiness.

3. **Time Management**
    - Effective Use of Time, Eliminate Time Wasters.
    - Be More Organised through Prioritisation.

4. **Effective Communication**
   - Communicate Effectively, Confidently and with Clarity.
   - Active Listening.
   - Improve Human Relations through Vertical and Horizontal Communication.

5. **Teamwork**
   - Build an Egoless Environment of Trust—Believe in and Accept Each Other.
   - Build an Efficient and Collaborative team.
   - Strengthen Group Dynamics.
   - Greater Buy-in in the Team—Voluntary Commitment.
   - Enhance Personal Productivity through Teamwork.
   - Harmony in the inter-functional relationship.

6. **Soft skills**
   - Create a Positive Environment.
   - Manage Anger and Stress to Be Happy.
   - Get out of your Comfort Zone
   - Handle Failure and Overcome Fear.
   - Develop Motivation, Self-Awareness, Self-Confidence, Responsibility and Accountability.
   - Be Empathetic.
   - Attention to Detail and Clarity of Thought.
   - Handling change in Customers' Expectations—External and Internal.

born towin®
learning services pvt. ltd

# About The Author

*Anand, a former Civil Servant in the Indirect Tax Administration, is committed to the 'Born To Win' methodology with conviction and faith. His transformation from a provider of solutions to a catalyst of change has been remarkable.*

*He has successfully implemented the "Born To Win" program for Enterprises all over India in the past 17 years. Using the Adult Learning format & focusing on Implementation, the process helps Individuals & Teams to enhance their performance on a sustained basis. "Delivering Results against pre-identified Metrics" for Enterprises is the USP of the "Born To Win" program.*

*Starting his professional life as a lecturer through civil service, he has now reinvented himself as a Coach, Mentor and Business Owner. He has a natural flair for Innovation, a Holistic Approach, Business Process Re-engineering.*

*He is a member of the Indian Society for Training & Development, the International Consulting Professional's Institute and the Business Network International and a Fellow of the All India Management Association.*

*He is enjoying his second innings, making a difference in people's lives with his Never-Say-Die Attitude.*